The Ultimate Hemp Cookbook

The Ultimate Hemp Cookbook

Matthew Petchinsky

The Ultimate Hemp Cookbook
By: Matthew Petchinsky

Disclaimer

This cookbook, *The Ultimate Hemp Cookbook*, is intended strictly for **educational and culinary purposes only**. It provides guidance for preparing foods that incorporate **culinary-grade hemp ingredients**, specifically those derived from the *Cannabis sativa L.* plant containing **no more than 0.3% THC by dry weight**—the legal threshold established under the 2018 United States Farm Bill and similar international regulations.

These recipes do **not** contain psychoactive properties, do **not** induce intoxication, and are **not intended to diagnose, treat, prevent, or cure any medical condition or disease**.

◈ **Legal Compliance**

The legal status of hemp-derived products can vary by country, state, or region. It is the **sole responsibility of the reader** to ensure that the possession, use, preparation, or consumption of hemp-based ingredients aligns with **all local, state, provincial, and federal laws or regulations** in their jurisdiction.

The author and publisher make no representations or warranties regarding the legal permissibility of hemp foods where you reside, nor are they liable for any legal consequences resulting from misuse.

◈ Health and Safety

While hemp is widely recognized for its nutritional benefits—including its content of plant-based proteins, essential fatty acids, fiber, and micronutrients—individuals should always **consult with a qualified healthcare professional** before introducing new dietary elements, especially if they:

- Have known or suspected food allergies
- Are pregnant or breastfeeding
- Have chronic medical conditions
- Are taking medications or undergoing treatment
- Are following a restricted or specialized diet

Each person's body is unique. Even non-psychoactive hemp ingredients may interact differently depending on health status or existing conditions.

◈ **Intended Use and Content Scope**

This book does **not** promote or endorse the recreational use of cannabis or any of its psychoactive forms. It also does **not** provide or imply medical advice, therapeutic treatment, or wellness prescriptions. The recipes herein are meant strictly for **culinary enjoyment, nutritional enrichment, and legal food experimentation**.

All ingredient descriptions are presented using general or culinary terminology. Branded products or dosage-specific language are **not used** to ensure the recipes remain compliant and accessible to a broad audience.

◇ Intended Audience

This cookbook is designed for use by adults who are **of legal age to purchase, possess, and consume hemp-derived food products** in their area. If you are unsure about the regulations that apply to you, please consult your local government or a legal expert before proceeding.

◈ Limitation of Liability

By using this cookbook, you accept full responsibility for your culinary choices, ingredient sourcing, food safety, and legal compliance. Neither the author, publisher, nor any affiliated parties shall be held liable for:

- Any physical or emotional harm resulting from the preparation or consumption of the recipes
- Legal complications resulting from improper use of hemp products
- Adverse reactions due to allergies, sensitivities, or misinterpretation of ingredients

Always handle food with care, use quality ingredients, and when in doubt—ask a professional.

Thank you for choosing *The Ultimate Hemp Cookbook*. Cook responsibly, legally, and with joy.

Introduction

Welcome to a New Culinary Era with Hemp

What if one of the most misunderstood plants on Earth turned out to be a **nutritional powerhouse**, an **eco-friendly ingredient**, and a surprisingly versatile **culinary companion**? That's the magic of **hemp**—and this cookbook is your guide to unlocking its full potential in your kitchen.

For centuries, hemp (*Cannabis sativa L.*) has been revered across cultures not for intoxication, but for its utility. From sails and rope to textiles, ink, and nutrition, hemp's role in history is vast and often forgotten. Today, modern science is rediscovering what ancient societies already knew: **hemp is an extraordinary plant** with the power to nourish the body, support sustainability, and elevate everyday meals.

◈ What This Cookbook Is (and Isn't)

This is not a cannabis cookbook.

You won't find psychoactive THC recipes here.

What you *will* find is a carefully curated collection of **35 delicious, non-psychoactive recipes** using **culinary-grade hemp ingredients**—from protein-rich hemp seeds and flour to hemp-seasoned dishes that will surprise your taste buds.

These recipes are:

- **Legal** under U.S. federal law (2018 Farm Bill compliant)
- **Non-intoxicating** and family-safe
- **Loaded with nutrition**, including essential amino acids, omega-3s, and plant-based fiber
- Created to **educate, empower, and delight** your senses

Whether you're frying up Southern-style hemp chicken, baking cinnamon-sugar snacks, or tossing together a quick hemp taco night, you're stepping into a world where **health meets flavor** and **tradition meets innovation**.

◈ Why Cook with Hemp?

Hemp ingredients—especially hemp hearts, hemp flour, and cold-pressed hemp oil—are:

- **Complete proteins** (they contain all 9 essential amino acids)
- **Excellent sources of omega-3 & omega-6 fatty acids**
- Naturally **gluten-free**, low in carbs, and rich in magnesium, zinc, and iron
- Ideal for plant-based, paleo, and whole-food diets

Plus, cooking with hemp helps reduce environmental impact. Hemp is one of the most sustainable crops in the world, requiring less water, no harsh pesticides, and absorbing more carbon dioxide per acre than most forests.

◈ **What You'll Discover Inside**

This book is divided into sections including:

- Crispy fried favorites (like hemp-battered chicken and onion rings)
- Sweet baked goods (donuts, muffins, churros)
- Satisfying mains (ribs, taco casseroles, seafood platters)
- Unique snacks and desserts infused with cinnamon, banana, chocolate, and more

Each recipe features:

- Easy-to-follow steps
- Ingredient substitutions for dietary needs
- **Fun Facts** exploring hemp's history, science, and cultural relevance

Whether you're a home chef, health enthusiast, or hemp-curious foodie, *The Ultimate Hemp Cookbook* gives you **flavorful, legal, and exciting ways to elevate your cooking**—while contributing to a more sustainable future.

Ready to cook with confidence and curiosity?

Turn the page—and let hemp lead the way.

RECIPE 1: Buttermilk Hemp Fried Chicken
Crispy, savory, and Southern-inspired with a hemp twist
Ingredients:

- 3–4 lbs chicken (legs, thighs, breasts)
- 2 cups buttermilk
- 2 cups seasoned hemp flour blend (or mix hemp flour with AP flour 1:1)
- 1 tsp paprika (optional)
- 1 tsp garlic powder
- 1 tsp onion powder
- Salt and pepper, to taste
- Oil for frying (vegetable or canola)

Instructions:

1. **Marinate**: Place chicken in a bowl with buttermilk. Cover and refrigerate for 1–8 hours to tenderize and flavor.
2. **Prepare Flour Mix**: In another bowl, whisk hemp flour blend with paprika, garlic powder, onion powder, salt, and pepper.
3. **Coat the Chicken**: Remove each piece from the buttermilk, let excess drip, and dredge in the seasoned flour until well coated.
4. **Heat Oil**: In a deep skillet or Dutch oven, heat oil to 350°F (175°C).
5. **Fry**: Fry chicken in batches, turning once, until golden brown and internal temp reaches 165°F (75°C), about 15–20 minutes.
6. **Drain and Serve**: Place on a wire rack or paper towels to drain. Serve hot with your favorite sides.

Tip:
For extra crunch, double dip by returning dredged chicken to the buttermilk and flour once more before frying.

◇ **Fun Fact:**

Hemp seeds contain all nine essential amino acids, making them one of the few complete plant proteins on Earth—ideal for athletes, vegans, and protein-conscious eaters.

◈ **RECIPE 2: Crispy Hemp Chicken Bites**
Perfect for snacking, dipping, or picky eaters
Ingredients:

- 1 lb boneless chicken breast or thighs
- 1 cup seasoned hemp flour
- 1 cup panko breadcrumbs
- 2 large eggs, beaten
- 1 tsp garlic powder
- 1 tsp onion powder
- Salt and pepper, to taste
- Oil for frying

Instructions:

1. **Prep Chicken**: Cut chicken into 1–2 inch chunks.
2. **Season Flour**: Mix hemp flour with garlic powder, onion powder, salt, and pepper.
3. **Dredge**: Dip each piece into hemp flour, then egg, then breadcrumbs.
4. **Fry**: In hot oil (350°F), fry in batches for 3–5 minutes per side until crispy and cooked through.
5. **Drain and Serve**: Drain on paper towels. Serve with dipping sauces like ranch, mustard, or sriracha mayo.

Tip:
Bake instead at 400°F (200°C) for 20 minutes, flipping halfway for a lower-fat version.

◈ **Fun Fact:**

In the 1700s, American colonists were required by law to grow hemp. It was vital for sails, rope, and even parchment paper.

◈ RECIPE 3: Hemp-Crusted Chicken Tenders
Golden, juicy tenders that everyone will love
Ingredients:

- 1 lb chicken tenderloins
- 1 cup buttermilk
- 1 cup seasoned hemp flour
- 1 tsp paprika
- 1 tsp garlic powder
- Salt and pepper
- Oil for frying

Instructions:

1. **Marinate**: Soak tenders in buttermilk for 30 minutes to overnight.
2. **Mix Flour**: Combine hemp flour with spices and seasonings.
3. **Dredge**: Remove chicken from buttermilk, dredge in flour mix.
4. **Fry**: Fry in 350°F oil for 4 minutes per side or until internal temp reaches 165°F.
5. **Drain and Serve**: Let cool on paper towels. Serve with ketchup, mustard, or garlic aioli.

Tip:
Want it extra crispy? Dip in buttermilk a second time and dredge again before frying.

◈ Fun Fact:
Hemp oil is rich in gamma-linolenic acid (GLA), a rare omega-6 fatty acid with anti-inflammatory properties not found in flax or chia.

◈ RECIPE 4: Southern-Style Chicken-Fried Hemp Steak
A comfort food classic made heartier with hemp
Ingredients:

- 4 cube steaks
- 1 cup seasoned hemp flour
- 1 tsp garlic powder
- 1 tsp onion powder
- 1 tsp paprika
- 2 eggs
- 1 cup buttermilk
- Salt and pepper
- Oil for frying

Gravy:

- ¼ cup hemp flour
- 2 cups whole milk
- Salt & pepper to taste

Instructions:

1. **Season** steaks with salt and pepper.
2. **Set Up Dredging**: Mix hemp flour and spices in one bowl. Beat eggs and buttermilk in another.
3. **Dredge**: Dip steaks into flour → egg mix → flour again.
4. **Fry**: Fry each steak in hot oil (medium-high heat) for 3–4 minutes per side.
5. **Make Gravy**: Reserve 2 tbsp oil and flour. Stir, add milk, and whisk until thickened.
6. **Serve**: Pour gravy over steak and enjoy with mashed potatoes or greens.

Tip:

Let breaded steaks rest 10 minutes before frying to help the coating adhere better.

◈ **Fun Fact:**

In early America, it's believed hemp paper was used for drafts of the Declaration of Independence. Whether myth or fact, hemp was certainly common for paper due to its strength.

◈ RECIPE 5: Garlic-Herb Hemp Butter Sauce

Flavor-packed and versatile on everything from veggies to pasta

Ingredients:

- 4 garlic cloves, minced
- ½ cup unsalted butter or olive oil
- 1 tsp hemp garlic salt (or regular salt + crushed hemp hearts)
- 1 tbsp lemon juice
- ½ tsp black pepper
- Optional: parsley or red pepper flakes

Instructions:

1. **Sauté Garlic**: Gently heat butter/oil over medium heat. Add garlic and sauté until fragrant.
2. **Season**: Stir in salt, pepper, and optional herbs.
3. **Finish**: Remove from heat and mix in lemon juice.
4. **Serve**: Drizzle over steak, vegetables, bread, or pasta.

Tip:

This sauce stores well in a glass jar in the fridge for 4–5 days. Reheat gently before serving.

◈ Fun Fact:

Hemp oil is a cold-pressed product and should never be used for high-heat cooking—but it's perfect in sauces, dips, or dressings for a nutty finish.

RECIPE 6: Fried Hemp Pickles
Crunchy, tangy, and perfect for game day or snacking
Ingredients:

- 1 jar dill pickle slices (16 oz), drained and patted dry
- 1 cup seasoned hemp flour
- 1 tsp paprika
- ½ tsp garlic powder
- Salt & black pepper
- 1 cup buttermilk
- 1 egg
- 2 cups panko breadcrumbs
- Oil for frying

Instructions:

1. **Dry the Pickles**: Lay slices on paper towels and blot dry to help coating stick.
2. **Prepare Dredging Stations**:
    - Bowl 1: hemp flour + spices
    - Bowl 2: beaten egg + buttermilk
    - Bowl 3: panko breadcrumbs
3. **Dredge** each pickle: flour → egg wash → breadcrumbs.
4. **Fry**: Heat oil to 375°F (190°C). Fry pickles in batches for 1–2 minutes per side.
5. **Drain & Serve**: Let cool on paper towels. Serve hot with ranch or garlic dip.

Tip:
Swap panko for crushed cornflakes or add hemp seeds to the breading for extra crunch.

◈ **Fun Fact:**

Hempcrete, a building material made from hemp and lime, is fire-resistant, carbon-negative, and naturally regulates moisture—perfect for eco-conscious construction.

◈ **RECIPE 7: Hemp-Crusted Onion Rings**
Light, golden, and ultra-crispy with a nutty hemp twist
Ingredients:

- 2 large yellow onions
- 1 cup seasoned hemp flour
- 1 tsp paprika
- ½ tsp garlic powder
- Salt & pepper
- 1 cup buttermilk
- 1 egg
- 2 cups breadcrumbs (panko or classic)
- Oil for frying

Instructions:

1. **Slice Onions** into thick rings and separate.
2. **Set Up Dredging**:
     - Flour + spices
     - Buttermilk + egg
     - Breadcrumbs
3. **Coat Each Ring**: flour → egg → breadcrumbs.
4. **Fry** at 375°F until golden (2–3 minutes per side).
5. **Drain** and serve hot with ketchup, aioli, or spicy dip.

Tip:
For crunchier rings, freeze coated onion rings for 15 minutes before frying.

◈ **Fun Fact:**
During the Renaissance, artists like Van Gogh and Rembrandt painted on hemp canvas due to its durability and resistance to rot—*canvas* comes from *cannabis*.

◈ RECIPE 8: Fried Hemp Mozzarella Sticks
Cheesy, melty, and made for dipping
Ingredients:

- 1 lb mozzarella cheese block, cut into sticks
- 1 cup seasoned hemp flour
- 2 eggs + 2 tbsp milk
- 2 cups breadcrumbs
- 1 tsp garlic powder
- 1 tsp onion powder
- Salt & pepper
- Oil for frying
- Marinara sauce for dipping

Instructions:

1. **Prep Cheese**: Cut mozzarella into ¾" x 4" sticks.
2. **Dredge**: flour → egg wash → breadcrumbs. Press well to coat.
3. **Freeze** for at least 2 hours. (This prevents oozing.)
4. **Fry** in 365°F oil for 1–2 minutes or until golden.
5. **Drain & Serve** with warm marinara or pesto.

Tip:
Double-dip for a thicker crust. Avoid overcrowding during frying.

◈ Fun Fact:
Hemp-derived CBD has been studied for its anticonvulsant effects. The FDA-approved drug *Epidiolex*, derived from hemp, is used to treat rare seizure disorders.

◈ RECIPE 9: Jalapeño Hemp-Ups (Fried Jalapeño Poppers)
Spicy, cheesy, and totally addictive
Ingredients:

- 12 jalapeños, halved and de-seeded
- 1 package (8 oz) cream cheese, softened
- 1 cup shredded cheddar
- 1 tsp garlic powder
- Salt & pepper
- 1 cup hemp flour
- 2 eggs, beaten
- 2 cups breadcrumbs
- Oil for frying

Instructions:

1. **Mix Filling**: Combine cream cheese, cheddar, garlic powder, salt, and pepper.
2. **Fill Peppers** generously with cheese mix.
3. **Dredge**: flour → egg → breadcrumbs.
4. **Chill**: Refrigerate for 30 mins to firm up.
5. **Fry** at 365°F for 3–4 minutes until golden and crisp.
6. **Serve** hot with ranch, chipotle mayo, or sour cream.

Tip:
Bake instead at 400°F for 20 minutes for a lighter version.

◈ Fun Fact:
Hemp absorbs more CO_2 than most trees—up to 15 tons per hectare—making it one of nature's top climate allies.

⬦ **RECIPE 10: Hemp Hot Seafood Platter**
Lightly fried shrimp, calamari, and whitefish with a golden hemp crust
Ingredients:

- ½ lb shrimp (peeled)
- ½ lb calamari rings
- ½ lb white fish (cod, tilapia), cut into chunks
- Salt & pepper
- Lemon wedges for serving

For the Batter:

- 1 cup hemp flour
- 1 tsp garlic powder
- 1 tsp paprika
- ½ tsp baking powder
- 1 cup cold water (or cold beer)
- Salt to taste
- Oil for deep frying

Instructions:

1. **Season Seafood** with salt and pepper.
2. **Prepare Batter**: Mix hemp flour, spices, and baking powder. Slowly whisk in water or beer until smooth.
3. **Heat Oil** to 375°F in deep fryer or skillet.
4. **Dip & Fry** seafood in batter, fry in batches until golden (2–4 minutes each).
5. **Drain** on paper towels. Serve hot with lemon wedges and sauce.

Tip:

Use beer for a lighter, crispier batter. Keep seafood dry before battering.

◈ Fun Fact:

Hemp paper predates wood pulp paper by centuries. The oldest known paper (circa 200 BCE) from China was made from hemp fiber.

RECIPE 11: Cinnamon Sugar Hemp Toast
A sweet breakfast classic with a nutritious hemp twist
Ingredients:

- 4 slices bread (white, whole grain, or sourdough)
- 2 tbsp butter, softened
- 2 tbsp sugar
- 1 tsp ground cinnamon
- 1 tsp ground hemp seeds (optional, for a nutty texture)

Instructions:

1. **Toast Bread** until golden in a toaster or on a skillet.
2. **Mix Topping**: Combine sugar, cinnamon, and hemp seeds.
3. **Butter the Toast** while warm.
4. **Sprinkle Generously** with the cinnamon-hemp sugar mixture.
5. **Serve Hot** and enjoy with coffee, fruit, or tea.

Tip:
Add banana slices or a drizzle of honey for extra richness.

◈ **Fun Fact:**
The word "canvas" comes from *cannabis*, because original artist canvases were made from durable hemp fibers.

◈ **RECIPE 12: Wake and Bake Hemp Pancakes**

Fluffy, warm pancakes infused with cinnamon and plant-powered goodness

Ingredients:

- 1½ cups all-purpose flour
- 3½ tsp baking powder
- 1 tbsp sugar
- 1 tsp salt
- 2 tsp ground cinnamon
- 1¼ cups milk
- 1 egg
- 3 tbsp melted butter
- 1 tsp vanilla extract
- Optional: 2 tbsp hemp seeds or ¼ cup mashed banana

Instructions:

1. **Combine Dry Ingredients**: In a large bowl, whisk flour, baking powder, sugar, salt, and cinnamon.
2. **Mix Wet Ingredients**: In a separate bowl, whisk milk, egg, butter, vanilla (and banana or hemp seeds, if using).
3. **Combine** wet and dry until just mixed (lumps are okay).
4. **Cook on Hot Griddle** over medium heat, using ¼ cup of batter per pancake.
5. **Flip When Bubbling**, cook another 1–2 minutes.
6. **Serve Hot** with syrup, berries, or nut butter.

Tip:

Don't overmix the batter—this keeps the pancakes fluffy.

◇ **Fun Fact:**

In 2700 BCE, Chinese Emperor Shen Nung used hemp in medicine for ailments like gout, malaria, and memory loss. Hemp has been food and medicine for millennia.

◈ RECIPE 13: Hemp Cinnamon French Toast

Golden on the outside, creamy inside, with a hemp-cinnamon finish

Ingredients:

- 8 slices day-old bread (brioche or challah preferred)
- 4 eggs
- ⅔ cup milk
- ¼ cup sugar
- 1 tsp vanilla extract
- 1 tsp cinnamon
- 1 tbsp ground hemp seeds
- Butter for frying
- Optional toppings: berries, maple syrup, powdered sugar

Instructions:

1. **Make Custard**: Whisk eggs, milk, sugar, vanilla, cinnamon, and hemp seeds.
2. **Dip Bread** quickly into the mixture—don't soak too long.
3. **Fry in Butter** over medium heat, about 2 minutes per side until golden.
4. **Serve Hot** with toppings of your choice.

Tip:

Use thick, slightly stale bread—it holds custard without falling apart.

◈ Fun Fact:

Hemp hearts (hulled seeds) are rich in iron and magnesium—both vital for energy production and blood oxygenation.

◈ RECIPE 14: Hemp Cinnamon Sugar Donuts (Baked)
Soft, spiced, and oven-baked for guilt-free indulgence
Ingredients:

- 1½ cups flour
- ½ cup sugar
- 1½ tsp baking powder
- ¼ tsp nutmeg
- ½ tsp salt
- ½ cup buttermilk
- 1 egg
- 1½ tbsp melted butter
- 1 tsp vanilla
- 2 tbsp cinnamon sugar (for coating)
- 1 tsp ground hemp seeds (optional)

Instructions:

1. **Preheat Oven** to 350°F (175°C). Grease a donut pan.
2. **Combine Dry Ingredients**: flour, sugar, baking powder, nutmeg, salt.
3. **Whisk Wet Ingredients**: buttermilk, egg, butter, vanilla.
4. **Mix Together** until just combined.
5. **Fill Donut Pan** ¾ full.
6. **Bake 8–10 Minutes** or until lightly golden.
7. **Cool Slightly**, then brush with butter and coat in cinnamon sugar.

Tip:
No donut pan? Use a muffin tin for donut holes.

◈ **Fun Fact:**

Hemp seeds have a 3:1 ratio of omega-6 to omega-3—considered optimal for human health, especially for reducing inflammation.

◈ RECIPE 15: Hemp Cinnamon Sugar Pretzels
Soft, chewy, and perfect with a warm sweet coating
Ingredients:

- 1½ cups warm water
- 1 tbsp sugar
- 2 tsp kosher salt
- 2¼ tsp active dry yeast
- 4½ cups flour
- 4 tbsp butter, melted
- 10 cups water
- ⅔ cup baking soda
- Cinnamon sugar mix (plus optional ground hemp seeds)

Instructions:

1. **Activate Yeast**: Combine warm water, sugar, and salt. Sprinkle in yeast, let foam (5 mins).
2. **Make Dough**: Mix with flour and melted butter. Knead until smooth.
3. **Let Rise**: Oil bowl, cover dough. Let rise for 1 hour or until doubled.
4. **Preheat Oven** to 450°F. Line baking sheets with parchment.
5. **Shape Pretzels**: Roll dough into ropes, form twists.
6. **Boil in Baking Soda Water** for 30 seconds each.
7. **Bake 12–14 Minutes** or until golden brown.
8. **Coat with Butter + Cinnamon Sugar** while warm.

Tip:
For a sweeter twist, drizzle with vanilla glaze or melted chocolate.

◈ Fun Fact:

Hemp's root system aerates the soil, replenishes nutrients, and requires little irrigation, making it a sustainable choice for farmers and foodies alike.

RECIPE 16: Baked Cinnamon Sugar Banana Chips
Naturally sweet, crispy, and perfect for snacking or lunchboxes
Ingredients:

- 2–3 ripe but firm bananas
- 2 tbsp lemon juice
- 2 tsp cinnamon sugar
- 1 tsp ground hemp seeds (optional)

Instructions:

1. **Preheat Oven** to 200°F (95°C). Line a baking sheet with parchment paper.
2. **Slice Bananas** into thin, even rounds (⅛" thick).
3. **Dip in Lemon Juice** to prevent browning. Drain excess.
4. **Arrange on Baking Sheet** in a single layer.
5. **Sprinkle with Cinnamon Sugar + Hemp Seeds**.
6. **Bake for 1.5–2 Hours**, flipping once halfway through, until golden and slightly crisp.
7. **Cool in Oven** with door slightly open to crisp further.
8. **Store in Airtight Jar** once fully cooled.

Tip:
The thinner the banana slices, the crispier the chips. Don't crowd the pan!

◈ **Fun Fact:**
Hemp seeds are loaded with tryptophan, a precursor to serotonin, which can help regulate mood and sleep.

⬦ RECIPE 17: Cinnamon Sugar Piecrust Cookies
Flaky, sweet, and a great use for leftover pie dough
Ingredients:

- 1¼ cups all-purpose flour
- ¼ tsp salt
- ½ cup cold unsalted butter, cubed
- ¼ cup ice water
- Cinnamon sugar for topping
- Optional: 1 tsp ground hemp seeds

Instructions:

1. **Make Dough**: Combine flour and salt. Cut in butter until crumbly. Slowly add ice water to form a soft dough.
2. **Chill Dough**: Wrap and refrigerate 30 minutes.
3. **Preheat Oven** to 350°F (175°C). Line a baking sheet.
4. **Roll Out Dough** to ¼" thickness. Cut into shapes.
5. **Top Each Cookie** with butter (optional) and sprinkle with cinnamon sugar and hemp seeds.
6. **Bake 8–10 Minutes** until edges are lightly golden.
7. **Cool on Rack** before serving.

Tip:
Brush with melted butter before sprinkling for a richer taste.

⬦ Fun Fact:
Hemp paper is more durable than wood pulp paper. It doesn't yellow with age, making it ideal for archival uses.

◈ RECIPE 18: Cinnamon Sugar Hemp Popcorn
A crunchy, sweet-salty snack with a hemp-powered upgrade
Ingredients:

- ½ cup popcorn kernels
- 2 tbsp oil (for stovetop) or air pop
- 2 tbsp melted butter
- 1 tbsp cinnamon sugar
- 1 tsp ground hemp seeds (optional)

Instructions:

1. **Pop the Corn** using preferred method (air popper or stovetop).
2. **Melt Butter** and drizzle over warm popcorn.
3. **Sprinkle with Cinnamon Sugar + Hemp Seeds.**
4. **Toss Gently** until evenly coated.
5. **Serve Fresh** or store in an airtight container.

Tip:
Use a large paper bag to shake and coat the popcorn evenly without crushing it.

◈ Fun Fact:
Hemp has been grown for over 10,000 years—longer than any other agricultural crop. It's one of humanity's oldest domesticated plants.

◈ RECIPE 19: Apple Cinnamon Hemp Muffins
Moist, spiced, and full of fruit with a hint of nutty depth
Ingredients:

- 2 cups flour
- ½ cup sugar
- 3 tsp baking powder
- ½ tsp salt
- 1 tsp cinnamon
- ½ cup ground hemp seeds or hemp flour
- 1 egg
- 1 cup milk
- ¼ cup butter, melted
- 1 tsp vanilla extract
- 1½ cups finely chopped apples

Instructions:

1. **Preheat Oven** to 400°F (200°C). Grease or line muffin tin.
2. **Mix Dry Ingredients** in a bowl: flour, sugar, baking powder, salt, cinnamon, hemp.
3. **In Separate Bowl**, beat egg, milk, melted butter, and vanilla.
4. **Combine Wet and Dry**, stir just until mixed.
5. **Fold in Apples** gently.
6. **Scoop into Muffin Tin**, filling each cup ⅔ full.
7. **Bake 15–20 Minutes** until golden and a toothpick comes out clean.
8. **Cool and Serve** with butter or hemp honey drizzle.

Tip:
Use tart apples like Granny Smith for the best flavor balance.

◇ **Fun Fact:**

Magnesium found in hemp seeds supports over 300 biochemical reactions in the body—including energy production and nerve function.

⬦ RECIPE 20: Cinnamon Sugar Hemp Bread

A quick loaf swirled with sweet spice and finished with a golden crust

Ingredients:

- 2 cups flour
- 1 tbsp baking powder
- ½ tsp salt
- 1 cup sugar
- 1 egg
- 1 cup milk
- ⅓ cup oil
- Cinnamon sugar mix (reserve half for swirl, half for topping)
- 2 tbsp ground hemp seeds (optional)

Instructions:

1. **Preheat Oven** to 350°F (175°C). Grease a 9x5″ loaf pan.
2. **Mix Dry Ingredients**: flour, baking powder, salt, sugar, hemp seeds.
3. **Combine Wet Ingredients**: egg, milk, oil.
4. **Combine Wet and Dry** until just mixed (don't overmix).
5. **Pour Half Batter** into pan, sprinkle half the cinnamon sugar.
6. **Add Remaining Batter** and swirl with a knife. Top with remaining sugar mix.
7. **Bake 45–50 Minutes** until a toothpick comes out clean.
8. **Cool in Pan**, then transfer to wire rack.

Tip:

Wrap tightly and enjoy the next day—it gets even more flavorful after resting.

◇ **Fun Fact:**

Hemp roots dig deep into the soil, helping prevent erosion and regenerate the land. It's a regenerative crop essential for the future of sustainable farming.

RECIPE 21: Hemp Cinnamon Churros
Golden and crisp on the outside, warm and soft inside—rolled in cinnamon hemp sugar
Ingredients:

- 1 cup water
- 2½ tbsp sugar
- ½ tsp salt
- 2 tbsp vegetable oil
- 1 cup all-purpose flour
- Oil for frying
- ½ cup cinnamon sugar mix
- 1 tbsp ground hemp seeds (optional)

Instructions:

1. **Make Dough**: In a saucepan, bring water, sugar, salt, and oil to a boil. Remove from heat and stir in flour until a smooth dough forms.
2. **Heat Oil** to 375°F (190°C) in a deep fryer or large pan.
3. **Pipe the Dough**: Transfer dough to a piping bag with a large star tip. Pipe 4–6 inch strips into the hot oil.
4. **Fry Until Golden**, about 2–4 minutes per side.
5. **Drain** on paper towels.
6. **Roll in Cinnamon-Hemp Sugar** while warm.

Tip:
For dipping, serve with melted chocolate, caramel, or a hemp vanilla glaze.

◈ **Fun Fact:**
Hemp grows in just 90–120 days, making it one of the fastest renewable crops in agriculture.

◈ RECIPE 22: Apple Cinnamon Stoner Muffins

Perfectly spiced and apple-packed with a soft crumb and earthy hemp note

Ingredients:

- 2 cups flour
- ½ cup sugar
- 3 tsp baking powder
- ½ tsp salt
- 1 tsp cinnamon
- ½ cup hemp flour or ground hemp seeds
- 1 egg
- 1 cup milk
- ¼ cup melted butter
- 1 tsp vanilla
- 1½ cups chopped apples

Instructions:

1. **Preheat Oven** to 400°F (200°C). Grease or line muffin pan.
2. **Mix Dry Ingredients**: flour, sugar, baking powder, salt, cinnamon, hemp.
3. **Whisk Wet Ingredients**: egg, milk, butter, vanilla.
4. **Combine Wet and Dry** just until moistened.
5. **Fold in Apples** gently.
6. **Spoon into Muffin Cups** and bake for 15–20 minutes.
7. **Cool Slightly**, then enjoy warm.

Tip:
Add chopped walnuts or raisins for texture and natural sweetness.

◈ Fun Fact:

Hemp seeds contain over 25% protein by weight—more than flax, chia, or quinoa.

◇ **RECIPE 23: Cinnamon Sugar Swirl Hemp Bread**

A comforting loaf swirled with spice and sprinkled with crunchy hemp topping

Ingredients:

- 2 cups flour
- 1 tbsp baking powder
- ½ tsp salt
- 1 cup sugar
- 1 egg
- 1 cup milk
- ⅓ cup vegetable oil
- 1 tbsp ground hemp seeds
- Cinnamon sugar mixture (for swirl and topping)

Instructions:

1. **Preheat Oven** to 350°F (175°C). Grease and flour a 9x5" loaf pan.
2. **Mix Dry Ingredients**: flour, baking powder, salt, sugar, hemp.
3. **Whisk Wet Ingredients**: egg, milk, oil.
4. **Combine** until just mixed—do not overmix.
5. **Layer Batter** in pan, adding cinnamon sugar in between and swirling with a knife.
6. **Top with More Cinnamon Sugar**.
7. **Bake 45–55 Minutes** or until golden and a toothpick comes out clean.
8. **Cool in Pan**, then slice and serve.

Tip:

Delicious toasted with a pat of butter or drizzle of maple syrup.

◇ **Fun Fact:**

George Washington and Thomas Jefferson both grew hemp—it was considered a staple American crop during the colonial era.

◈ RECIPE 24: Hemp Cinnamon Sugar Popcorn

A crunchy, lightly sweetened snack perfect for cozy nights or party bowls

Ingredients:

- ½ cup popcorn kernels
- 2 tbsp coconut or vegetable oil (for stovetop)
- 2 tbsp melted butter
- 1 tbsp cinnamon sugar
- 1 tsp ground hemp seeds (optional)

Instructions:

1. **Pop the Popcorn** via air popper or stovetop.
2. **Drizzle with Melted Butter.**
3. **Sprinkle with Cinnamon Sugar + Hemp Seeds.**
4. **Toss to Coat** evenly.
5. **Serve Fresh** or store in an airtight container.

Tip:
Try a pinch of cayenne for a spicy-sweet twist!

◈ Fun Fact:

Hemp is one of the only plants that can regenerate soil by removing toxins and restoring nutrients—used in phytoremediation.

◈ RECIPE 25: Cinnamon Sugar Pie Crust Cookies
Flaky, buttery, and golden with a crunchy sugar-hemp topping

Ingredients:

- 1¼ cups all-purpose flour
- ¼ tsp salt
- ½ cup chilled unsalted butter, diced
- ¼ cup ice water
- 2 tbsp melted butter (for brushing)
- Cinnamon sugar mix
- 1 tbsp ground hemp seeds

Instructions:

1. **Make the Dough**: Blend flour, salt, and butter until crumbly. Add water gradually until a dough forms.
2. **Chill 30 Minutes**, then roll out to ¼ inch thick.
3. **Preheat Oven** to 350°F (175°C). Line a baking sheet.
4. **Cut into Shapes** using cookie cutters.
5. **Brush with Butter**, sprinkle with cinnamon sugar and hemp.
6. **Bake 8–10 Minutes** or until lightly golden.
7. **Cool on Rack** and enjoy.

Tip:
This is a perfect way to use leftover pie dough scraps!

◈ Fun Fact:
Hemp is naturally pest-resistant, reducing the need for chemical pesticides and herbicides in farming.

RECIPE 26: Hemp Cinnamon Banana Bread Muffins
Moist, hearty, and warmly spiced with a nutty hemp boost
Ingredients:

- 1½ cups flour
- ½ cup hemp flour or ground hemp seeds
- 1 tsp baking soda
- 1 tsp baking powder
- ½ tsp salt
- 1 tsp cinnamon
- ½ cup butter, melted
- ¾ cup brown sugar
- 2 large ripe bananas, mashed
- 2 eggs
- 1 tsp vanilla extract

Instructions:

1. **Preheat Oven** to 350°F (175°C). Line or grease a muffin tin.
2. **Mix Dry Ingredients**: flour, hemp, baking soda, baking powder, salt, cinnamon.
3. **In Another Bowl**, whisk melted butter, sugar, bananas, eggs, and vanilla.
4. **Combine Wet and Dry** until just mixed.
5. **Divide Batter** evenly between 12 muffin cups.
6. **Bake 18–22 Minutes** or until a toothpick comes out clean.
7. **Cool and Enjoy** with tea or as a grab-and-go breakfast.

Tip:
Add chopped walnuts, chocolate chips, or dried fruit for extra texture and flavor.

◈ **Fun Fact:**

Banana + hemp = a magnesium powerhouse! Together they promote muscle relaxation, brain function, and calm mood.

◈ **RECIPE 27: Hemp Honey Butter Biscuits**
Fluffy, golden biscuits infused with rich hemp seeds and sweet honey butter
Ingredients:

- 2 cups flour
- 1 tbsp baking powder
- ½ tsp baking soda
- ½ tsp salt
- ½ cup cold butter, cubed
- ¾ cup cold buttermilk
- ¼ cup ground hemp seeds

Honey Butter:

- 3 tbsp butter, softened
- 2 tbsp honey
- Pinch of cinnamon

Instructions:

1. **Preheat Oven** to 425°F (220°C). Line a baking sheet.
2. **Mix Dry Ingredients**: flour, baking powder, baking soda, salt, hemp.
3. **Cut in Butter** until mixture resembles coarse crumbs.
4. **Add Buttermilk** and stir until dough forms.
5. **Pat Dough** to ¾-inch thick and cut biscuits with a round cutter.
6. **Bake 12–15 Minutes** until golden.
7. **Whip Honey Butter** ingredients and serve on warm biscuits.

Tip:
Freeze shaped biscuits before baking for fresh-baked flavor any time.

◈ **Fun Fact:**

Hemp is a source of GLA (gamma-linolenic acid), a rare omega-6 that supports hormone balance and healthy skin.

◈ **RECIPE 28: Twisted Cinnamon Hemp Ice Cream Sandwiches**

Cool, creamy, and nestled between soft cinnamon cookies
Ingredients (Cookies):

- 1 cup butter, softened
- 1 cup brown sugar
- 2 eggs
- 2 cups flour
- 1 tsp baking soda
- 1 tsp cinnamon
- ½ tsp salt
- ½ cup ground hemp seeds

Filling:

- 1 pint vanilla or cinnamon ice cream (dairy or non-dairy)

Instructions:

1. **Preheat Oven** to 350°F (175°C). Line a baking sheet.
2. **Cream Butter + Sugar**, add eggs one at a time.
3. **Mix Dry Ingredients**, then combine with wet until a soft dough forms.
4. **Drop Dough** by spoonfuls and flatten slightly.
5. **Bake 10–12 Minutes**. Cool completely.
6. **Scoop Ice Cream** onto one cookie, top with another, and press gently.
7. **Freeze Sandwiches** 1–2 hours before serving.

Tip:
Roll sandwich edges in crushed nuts, mini chips, or cinnamon sugar.

◈ **Fun Fact:**

Hemp seeds contain stearidonic acid (SDA), a rare omega-3 that's even more easily converted by the body than flax oil.

◈ **RECIPE 29: Toasted Hemp Apple Crumble**
Warm, spiced apples baked under a crisp cinnamon-hemp oat topping
Ingredients:
Filling:

- 5 apples, peeled and sliced
- 2 tbsp lemon juice
- ¼ cup sugar
- 1 tsp cinnamon
- 1 tbsp flour

Topping:

- ¾ cup oats
- ½ cup flour
- ½ cup brown sugar
- ½ cup cold butter, diced
- ⅓ cup hemp seeds
- ½ tsp cinnamon

Instructions:

1. **Preheat Oven** to 375°F (190°C). Grease a baking dish.
2. **Toss Apples** with lemon juice, sugar, cinnamon, and flour. Spread in dish.
3. **Mix Topping** ingredients until crumbly.
4. **Sprinkle Topping** over apples.
5. **Bake 35–40 Minutes** or until bubbling and golden.
6. **Cool Slightly** before serving with ice cream or whipped cream.

Tip:

For tart flavor, use Granny Smith apples. Add chopped walnuts for crunch.

◈ **Fun Fact:**

Oats + hemp make a blood-sugar-friendly combo: high in fiber, protein, and healthy fats that stabilize energy.

◈ RECIPE 30: No-Bake Cinnamon Hemp Energy Bites

Sweet, satisfying snacks that pack protein, fiber, and flavor in one bite

Ingredients:

- 1 cup rolled oats
- ½ cup ground hemp seeds
- ½ cup nut butter (peanut, almond, or sunflower)
- ¼ cup honey or maple syrup
- 1 tsp cinnamon
- 1 tsp vanilla
- Pinch of salt
- Optional: ¼ cup mini chocolate chips or raisins

Instructions:

1. **Mix All Ingredients** in a large bowl until evenly combined.
2. **Chill Mixture** in fridge for 15–20 minutes to firm up.
3. **Roll into Balls** about 1-inch wide.
4. **Store in Fridge** in airtight container for up to 1 week.

Tip:

These freeze beautifully. Great for post-workout, lunchboxes, or dessert.

◈ Fun Fact:

Hemp protein contains edestin, a highly digestible globular protein rarely found in other plants—ideal for nutrient absorption.

RECIPE 31: Hemp Cinnamon Raisin Bread

A tender breakfast loaf bursting with raisins and warming spice

Ingredients:

- 3 cups all-purpose flour
- 1 tbsp ground hemp seeds
- 1 tsp salt
- ¼ cup sugar
- 1 tbsp active dry yeast
- 1 cup warm water (110°F)
- 2 tbsp butter, melted
- 1 tsp cinnamon
- 1 cup raisins

Instructions:

1. **Activate Yeast**: Combine warm water, sugar, and yeast. Let sit 5–10 mins until foamy.
2. **Combine Flour, Salt, Cinnamon, and Hemp** in a large bowl.
3. **Mix Wet and Dry** until a soft dough forms. Add melted butter and knead until smooth (about 5–7 mins).
4. **Fold in Raisins**, knead gently to incorporate.
5. **Let Rise** in greased bowl, covered, 1 hour.
6. **Shape into Loaf**, place in greased 9x5" loaf pan. Rise again 30–45 mins.
7. **Bake at 375°F (190°C)** for 30–35 minutes.
8. **Cool and Slice** for breakfast or snacking.

Tip:

Brush top with melted butter and cinnamon sugar before baking for a caramelized crust.

◇ **Fun Fact:**

Hemp was used in early American currency paper—durable, water-proof, and long-lasting.

◇ RECIPE 32: Fluffy Hemp Protein Pancakes

Perfect post-workout pancakes packed with plant-based protein

Ingredients:

- 1 cup flour
- ½ cup hemp protein powder or ground hemp seeds
- 2 tbsp sugar
- 1 tsp baking powder
- ½ tsp baking soda
- ½ tsp salt
- 1 cup milk or plant milk
- 1 egg
- 2 tbsp oil or melted butter
- 1 tsp vanilla

Instructions:

1. **Combine Dry Ingredients** in a mixing bowl.
2. **In a Separate Bowl**, mix milk, egg, oil, and vanilla.
3. **Whisk Together** until just combined.
4. **Preheat Griddle** to medium heat. Grease lightly.
5. **Pour Batter** (¼ cup each) and cook until bubbles form.
6. **Flip and Cook** until both sides are golden.
7. **Serve Hot** with cinnamon syrup, yogurt, or nut butter.

Tip:

Add blueberries, sliced banana, or chocolate chips for variety.

◇ Fun Fact:

Hemp protein includes all nine essential amino acids—making it a complete plant protein.

◈ **RECIPE 33: Spiced Hemp Cupcakes with Cinnamon Frosting**

Decadent, cozy cupcakes with a hint of spice and a creamy hemp-cinnamon finish

Ingredients (Cupcakes):

- 1½ cups flour
- ½ cup ground hemp seeds
- 1 tsp baking powder
- ½ tsp baking soda
- ½ tsp salt
- 1 tsp cinnamon
- ½ cup butter, softened
- ¾ cup brown sugar
- 2 eggs
- 1 tsp vanilla
- ½ cup milk

Frosting:

- ½ cup butter, softened
- 1½ cups powdered sugar
- 1 tsp cinnamon
- 1–2 tbsp milk or cream

Instructions:

1. **Preheat Oven** to 350°F (175°C). Line cupcake tin.
2. **Cream Butter + Sugar**, then add eggs and vanilla.
3. **Mix Dry Ingredients**, then alternate adding with milk to wet ingredients.
4. **Scoop Batter** into liners ¾ full.
5. **Bake 15–18 Minutes**, cool completely before frosting.
6. **Whip Frosting** until fluffy and frost with a swirl.

Tip:
Top with crushed hemp seeds or a dusting of cinnamon sugar for flair.

◈ Fun Fact:
The U.S. Declaration of Independence was drafted on hemp paper—durable and anti-fungal.

◈ RECIPE 34: Warm Hemp Cinnamon Rice Pudding

Comforting, creamy dessert or breakfast with earthy notes and spice

Ingredients:

- 1 cup cooked white or jasmine rice
- 2 cups milk (or plant milk)
- ¼ cup sugar or maple syrup
- ½ tsp cinnamon
- ¼ tsp nutmeg
- 1 tsp vanilla
- Pinch of salt
- 2 tbsp hemp seeds

Instructions:

1. **Combine All Ingredients** in a saucepan.
2. **Simmer on Low Heat**, stirring often for 20–25 mins until thickened.
3. **Serve Warm or Chilled**, sprinkled with extra cinnamon and hemp seeds.

Tip:

Add raisins, chopped apples, or toasted coconut for texture.

◈ Fun Fact:

Hemp seeds are easier to digest than soy or whey and are naturally lactose-free—ideal for gentle gut support.

⬦ RECIPE 35: Cinnamon Hemp Bread Pudding

A rich dessert that transforms stale bread into a soft, cinnamon-kissed masterpiece

Ingredients:

- 5 cups cubed day-old bread (French or brioche)
- 2 cups milk or plant milk
- 3 eggs
- ½ cup sugar
- 1 tsp cinnamon
- 1 tsp vanilla
- ¼ tsp salt
- 2 tbsp hemp seeds
- Optional: raisins or chopped nuts

Instructions:

1. **Preheat Oven** to 350°F (175°C). Grease an 8x8" dish.
2. **Whisk Eggs, Milk, Sugar, Cinnamon, Vanilla, Salt** in a large bowl.
3. **Add Bread Cubes**, toss gently to soak.
4. **Let Sit** 10 minutes for full absorption.
5. **Pour into Dish**, sprinkle with hemp seeds and optional toppings.
6. **Bake 35–40 Minutes** or until set and golden.
7. **Serve Warm** with whipped cream or maple drizzle.

Tip:

Use a mix of breads (white, whole grain, cinnamon raisin) for complexity.

⬦ **Fun Fact:**

Hemp is one of the few edible seeds with a perfect balance of omega-6 to omega-3 fatty acids—ideal for heart and brain health.